I0042589

Informal Entrepreneurship and Cross-Border Trade between Zimbabwe and South Africa

Abel Chikanda and Godfrey Tawodzera

SAMP MIGRATION POLICY SERIES NO. 74

Series Editor: Prof. Jonathan Crush

Southern African Migration Programme (SAMP)

2017

AUTHORS

Abel Chikanda is Assistant Professor of Geography and African & African American Studies, University of Kansas, Lawrence, Kansas, United States.

Godfrey Tawodzera is Senior Lecturer, Department of Geography, University of Limpopo, Polokwane, South Africa.

ACKNOWLEDGEMENTS

SAMP and its partners acknowledge the support of the IDRC for funding the Growing Informal Cities Project. The following are thanked for their assistance in the preparation of the report for publication: Jonathan Crush, Bronwen Dachs and Maria Salamone. Further thanks to Paul Okwi and Edgard Rodriguez of IDRC.

Published by the Southern African Migration Programme, International Migration Research Centre, Balsillie School of International Affairs, Waterloo, Ontario, Canada, and the African Centre for Cities, University of Cape Town, Cape Town, South Africa

First published 2017

ISBN 978-1-920596-29-3

Cover photo: Africa Media Online

Production by Bronwen Dachs Muller, Cape Town

Printed by Print on Demand, Cape Town

All rights reserved. No part of this publication may be reproduced or transmitted, in any form or by any means, without prior permission from the publishers

CONTENTS

PAGE

LIST OF TABLES

LIST OF FIGURES

EXECUTIVE SUMMARY

Zimbabwe has witnessed the rapid expansion of informal cross-border trading (ICBT) with neighbouring countries over the past two decades. Beginning in the mid-1990s when the country embarked on its Economic Structural Adjustment Programme (ESAP), a large number of people were forced into informal employment through worsening economic conditions and the decline in formal sector jobs. The country's post-2000 economic collapse resulted in the closure of many industries and created market opportunities for the further expansion of ICBT.

This report, part of SAMP's Growing Informal Cities series, sought to provide a current picture of ICBT in Zimbabwe by interviewing a sample of 514 Harare-based informal entrepreneurs involved in cross-border trading with South Africa. Traders who met the following criteria were selected for interview: (a) trading in the informal sector and not registered for tax purposes; (b) in operation for at least a year to allow for a retrospective analysis of start-up, problems and opportunities; and (c) conducting business primarily between Harare and Johannesburg. In addition, 24 in-depth interviews as well as two focus group discussions were held with the cross-border traders in Harare.

ICBT in Zimbabwe remains a female-dominated activity, and women made up 68% of this sample. Furthermore, traders exhibit a relatively youthful profile, with a mean age of 33 years in this sample. Cross-border traders are generally well educated, with 66% of the sample holding a high school diploma, and 14% having post-secondary educational qualifications. Nearly 90% of the respondents interviewed had started their businesses in the post-2000 era. Most had never held a formal job and went into ICBT either because they were unemployed or already involved in informal sector activities in Zimbabwe. Seventy percent of the traders rely on ICBT only for survival and have no other sources of income.

An examination of motivation to start an ICBT business shows that even though some took it up only out of economic necessity, many saw opportunities here. The initial capital used to start the business was low, with almost three-quarters of the sample having used ZAR5,000 or less. Most of the traders acquired their start-up capital from personal sources; nearly 60% used their personal savings and another 38% borrowed money from relatives to enable them to get going. When they need funds to expand their business or meet other business costs, they rely on their personal networks to obtain loans. Formal loan sources such as banks or other formal financial institutions are rarely used, either because of the high interest rates or stringent conditions attached to obtaining loans.

On average, the ICBT traders are highly mobile, spending only 1.8 days in South Africa on average per visit, although some stay for several weeks (particularly if they are taking goods to sell). The traders travel relatively frequently to South Africa, with 67% making at least one trip a month and 82% travelling more than four times a year. The vast majority do not have their own means of transport and rely on bus services. In Johannesburg, the traders purchase their goods at a small number of outlets especially China Mall (26%), other Chinese-run malls (25%) and Oriental Plaza (5%). By far the most common items bought in South Africa are new clothing and shoes (bought by 88%). Other goods include accessories such as bags and suitcases (bought by 27%), bedding materials (20%), electronics (12%) and household products (8%). In the past, ICBT was important in moving foodstuffs to Zimbabwe, but that is no longer the case.

The traders make important contributions to both the Zimbabwean and South African economies. Their positive impact on Zimbabwe includes:

- ICBT traders service the needs of Zimbabwean consumers either by providing goods that are unavailable in the country or at cheaper prices than similar goods supplied by local producers and the formal retail sector.

- ICBT enterprises contribute to the economy through business establishment, growth and the strategic deployment of their profits. The reported profits averaged ZAR4,765 per month but were highly variable, ranging from a minimum of ZAR200 per month to a maximum of ZAR45,000 per month. These profits indicate that ICBT is not just a survivalist enterprise, but a business operation where sizable profits can be made.

- Business profits are used to support families, with one-third (32%) spending their profits on family needs, including paying rent for accommodation, buying food for the family and other obligatory family expenses. Another 15% use their profits for education (such as school fees for dependants) and 14% spend the funds on themselves.

- ICBT traders contribute to Zimbabwe's economy through job creation. A total of 37% of the traders employ people in Zimbabwe as part of their business. Of the 308 people employed in the enterprises surveyed, 236 (or 77%) were in paid positions. Even when members of the family are involved in the business, they tend to be compensated for their time. Of the 128 family members employed, 71% were in paid positions. As many as 61% of the paid jobs went to non-family members.

- Job creation in the businesses set up by the traders is heavily female-oriented. Of the 236 paid employees in this study, 72% were women.

- Other beneficiaries include the Zimbabwean bus companies and the general Zimbabwean fiscus, which benefits from duties levied at the border on returning traders bringing in products with a value above the duty free limit. On their last trip to South Africa, the ICBT traders paid ZAR431 on average in customs duties, which amounts to ZAR228,529 levied in one trip by these 500 traders alone.

In South Africa, the positive impacts of ICBT from Zimbabwe are also felt in several ways:

- The greatest beneficiaries are the South African wholesalers from whom the traders purchase their goods. The traders also support the South African transport and hospitality industries.

- Overall, these traders spent an average of ZAR8,039 on their last trip to South Africa. The spend on particular items included ZAR6,737 on goods (or ZAR3.5 million in total), ZAR683 on transportation (ZAR361,000 in total), ZAR42 on accommodation (ZAR22,000 in total) and ZAR141 on other costs.

- South Africa benefits from the value added tax (VAT) paid by the traders. Visitors to South Africa who buy goods for use in their home country are eligible to apply for a VAT refund when they exit the country. However, only 22% of the cross-border traders reported that they claimed VAT back at the border.

The traders face a wide range of problems including queues and delays at the border, experienced often by 74% and sometimes by 23% of the respondents, and high duties levied at the border (60% said they often experience this problem). Other challenges include competition from other traders (experienced often/sometimes by 84%) and competition from large retailers or supermarkets (experienced often/sometimes by 60%). Xenophobia in South Africa is not as great a challenge to the operations of the ICBT traders as it is to Zimbabweans living in South Africa and running a business there. As many as 78% said they have not been affected by xenophobia at all in their business operations, while only 4% have been affected a great deal. Almost an equal number (30% in Zimbabwe and 28% in South Africa respectively) had been robbed, which indicates that the traders are at risk of crime in both countries, primarily because their business is cash-based.

The report concludes that ICBT has become more than a survivalist strategy and is now an important pillar of the Zimbabwean economy. The contribution of the informal economy in generating jobs and reducing unemployment needs to be acknowledged by policies that encourage rather than restrict the operation of informal trade.

INTRODUCTION

In June 2016, the government of Zimbabwe, through Statutory Instrument 64 of 2016, banned the importation of a wide variety of goods including various processed and tinned foods, bottled water, dairy products, household furniture, fertilizer, cotton fabric and some building materials. According to the Minister of Industry and Commerce, the move was designed "to support our local industry…buying locally manufactured goods; whether it involves purchasing machinery worth millions or even just a T-shirt; begins a cycle in which you re-invest money into the local economy, instead of spending it on an imported product and sending the money outbound."[1] The announcement triggered widespread protests by informal cross-border traders in Harare and at the Beitbridge border post between Zimbabwe and South Africa. The ostensible reason for the response was that the livelihoods of many in the informal economy, who make a living importing goods from South Africa and Botswana, were under threat by the state.[2] And the informal economy itself is the primary, and for many the only, source of income for households in the country.

A recent study has estimated that there are as many as 3.5 million micro, small and medium enterprises (MSMEs) in Zimbabwe.[3] Of these, 2 million (or 71%) are individual entrepreneurs and 800,000 (29%) have employees. Forty-six percent of the adult population nationally are MSME owners (as are 38% in Harare). Nearly half report that the business is their only source of income. Hours are long and hard with 50% working eight hours or more per day and 69% working six or seven days per week. In total, 53% are women. The MSMEs employ a total of 2.9 million additional people of whom 22% are full-time paid, 26% are paid temporary workers and 22% are unpaid (primarily family members). As many as 85% are not registered or licensed, and are therefore operating in the informal economy. Only 14% use banks and other formal financial products and services and just 3% have a business bank account. Unfortunately, the study does not indicate how many MSMEs are involved in cross-border trading but the numbers are probably substantial.

Cross-border trading is a well-established entrepreneurial activity throughout the Southern African Development Community (SADC), accounting for 30-40% of intra-regional trade.[4] ICBT not only expands the market for Zimbabwean goods (such as handicrafts) but also facilitates the import of a wide variety of perishables and non-perishables to sell to the Zimbabwean consumer. ICBT as a household livelihood strategy grew rapidly in the 1990s under the impact of the country's Economic Structural Adjustment Programme

(ESAP).[5] The austerity measures implemented under ESAP resulted in the closure of many industries due to the removal of subsidies and increased import costs after the devaluation of the currency. While these measures were aimed at streamlining government expenditure and stimulating growth, thousands of workers were rendered jobless. They entered the informal sector in growing numbers and ICBT was one of the activities that redundant workers turned to for survival. At that time, the business was dominated by female traders.[6] Although South Africa imposed tough visa restrictions on Zimbabweans after 1995, cross-border trading increasingly became a way for households to secure a livelihood.

The government's assault on all forms of urban informality in 2005 in the form of Operation Murambatsvina temporarily interrupted the trade, but it quickly re-established itself as the participants had few viable alternatives and South Africa had meanwhile lifted its visa requirements on temporary entrants.[7] In 2007, at the height of Zimbabwe's economic crisis, SAMP conducted a border monitoring study of informal traders at four major border posts and found that the trade was increasing and diversifying, and that more men were becoming involved.[8] As Zimbabwe's shops emptied and the purchasing power of the Zimbabwean dollar evaporated during the economic meltdown of 2008, ICBT traders played a critical role in ensuring that essential supplies, such as foodstuffs, remained accessible to many households. The volume of informal trade at the Zimbabwean borders with South Africa and Botswana reached record proportions during the crisis.[9] While the informal economy has traditionally been viewed with suspicion by the Zimbabwean government and local authorities, there is no denying that it is this sector of the economy that has kept the country afloat in economically difficult times. Understanding the nature of its contribution is to acknowledge the significant and indispensable role of this otherwise undervalued sector of the economy.

The political and economic stabilization of Zimbabwe after 2009 with the formation of a Government of National Unity was short-lived and the country's economic situation has deteriorated again. However, there is the question of what, if any, impact the period of economic stability following the crisis of 2007-2008 had on ICBT. On the one hand, many goods that were formerly unavailable in the country returned to the shops. On the other, formal sector unemployment remained stubbornly high and many households continued to rely on the informal economy for their livelihoods.[10] With this in mind, the Growing Informal Cities project set out to provide an updated picture of ICBT between Zimbabwe and South Africa by interviewing in Harare a sample of informal entrepreneurs involved in ICBT with South Africa.

This report begins with a discussion of the methodology used to identify and interview the ICBT traders. The second section presents a socio-demographic profile of the traders including their age, sex, marital status and educational level. The section also discusses what occupations the traders were involved in before taking up cross-border trade, when they started their businesses, and any other income-generating activities in which they were involved. The third section addresses the question of whether the traders were pushed into the business just to survive or had other entrepreneurial motivations. The report then examines the business strategies and challenges faced by ICBT traders and concludes with a discussion of the positive economic implications of ICBT trade for both South Africa and Zimbabwe. In light of this discussion, it is clear that attempts to rigorously control and even eliminate the trade are counter-productive for both countries.

RESEARCH METHODOLOGY

This research employed both qualitative and quantitative techniques to obtain a profile of cross-border traders and insights into their motivation, operations, challenges and opportunities. A detailed questionnaire developed by the GIC-SAMP partners was administered to a total of 534 ICBT traders in Harare. Only traders who met the following criteria were selected: (a) trading in the informal sector and not registered for tax purposes; (b) in operation for at least one year to allow for a retrospective analysis of the start-up, problems and opportunities; and (c) conducting business primarily between Harare and Johannesburg. Only those who actually travel between Harare and Johannesburg (rather than other members of the business involved in either sourcing or selling the goods in Harare) were selected for interviews.

Because it is impossible to draw a representative sample of cross-border traders, the study adopted a snowball sampling strategy. This involved identifying a small group of cross-border traders in multiple locations across Harare. These traders were then used as initial sampling units and were asked to identify other traders to be included in the sample. Each interviewed cross-border trader was asked to identify at least three other traders and, from these, one was randomly selected for interview. The process was repeated until the desired sample size was achieved.

The questionnaires were administered in 10 areas in Harare, including Chitungwiza and Epworth. Half of the sample was from the Harare CBD where the areas sampled included

Fourth, Cameroon, Chinhoyi, Kwame Nkrumah, and Mbuya Nehanda streets, as well as traders located at the Food World, Charge Office, Copa Cabana, and the Gulf Complex flea markets. Outside the CBD, cross-border traders were interviewed in Mbare and Muped-zanhamo (21%), Chitungwiza town centre, Makoni and St Mary's (7%), Highfield and Machipisa (6%), Avondale (4%), Epworth (2%) and Kuwadzana (3%) (Table 1).

Table 1: Sampled Areas of Harare

	No.	%
Harare CBD	263	49.6
Mbare and Mupedzanhamo	110	20.6
Chitungwiza, Makoni and St Mary's	36	6.7
Highfield and Machipisa	33	6.1
Avondale	20	3.7
Kuwadzana 4, 5 and 7	17	3.2
Warren Park 1	15	2.8
Epworth	12	2.2
Glen View 3, 7 and 8	12	2.2
Mabvuku – Tafara	12	2.2
Other	4	0.7
Total	534	100.0

Because of the complexity of ICBT, it is possible that some trading activities were not captured in the survey. Those operating home-based businesses and those selling to inter-mediaries may be under-represented, for example. These limitations notwithstanding, the size of the sample from across the city is likely to give a generally accurate picture of Harare's cross-border traders. The questionnaire collected information on such issues as the profile of those involved in cross-border trading enterprises; when the enterprise was started; the motivation for engaging in ICBT; the nature of the enterprises and goods traded; the num-ber of people employed; their ownership structure, capitalization, income and growth; and the problems the traders face in operating their businesses in Zimbabwe and South Africa.

Twenty-four in-depth interviews were conducted with selected cross-border traders in Harare. A semi-structured interview schedule was used for the interviews. The interviews enabled the researchers to probe and better understand the origins and contemporary context of ICBT. The interviews addressed key issues by exploring the journey of the traders from Zimbabwe to South Africa and back; the problems they face; how they surmount some of these challenges; and the opportunities they see in expanding their businesses and making a contribution to the country's economy.

Two focus group discussions were held in Harare with groups of traders in the city centre. The first group consisted of seven cross-border traders of which five were women and two were men. The second focus group discussion consisted of six cross-border traders: four women and two men. The discussions focused on understanding the motivation for venturing into ICBT; the nature of the trade; how traders traverse informal trading spaces; their relationships with local authorities and the police; the sourcing of capital for their businesses; and their everyday challenges and opportunities.

A number of in-depth interviews were also conducted with key informants in the city, including representatives of trader organizations. The selection of informants was based on their ability to supply information relevant to cross-border trading and issues related to the operation of these enterprises. Some were able to address questions on motivation for entering cross-border trading, challenges experienced in the trade, opportunities within the environments of cross-border trading, and trajectories of the trade in the future.

PROFILE OF ICBT ENTREPRENEURS

ICBT from Zimbabwe has traditionally been dominated by female traders with limited involvement of men.[11] In Southern Africa as a whole, women make up an estimated 70-80% of informal cross-border traders.[12] The majority of traders interviewed in this study were women (68%). The sample was also relatively young, with a mean age of 33 years. The dominance of young people in cross-border trading is explained by the arduous nature of the trade, which involves a great deal of travelling and considerable time spent waiting at border posts and where goods are sourced. The 1,200 km trip from Harare to Johannesburg normally takes 18-20 hours on public transport, of which 3-6 hours are spent at the border post between Zimbabwe and South Africa. Although the maximum age recorded for a trader in this survey was 72, very few were over 60.

Cross-border trade in the 1990s was associated with the less educated and unskilled.[13] This Harare sample was better educated with only 1% of the sample not having completed primary school (Figure 1). Two-thirds had a high school diploma, while another 17% had some secondary level education. Some traders had a college certificate or diploma (11%) while 2% had undergraduate degrees and 1% a postgraduate degree. The entry of better-educated people in ICBT is certainly a result of continuing high unemployment levels in Zimbabwe. However, the trade is still dominated by individuals without higher education.

Figure 1: Highest Level of Education Completed by ICBT Traders

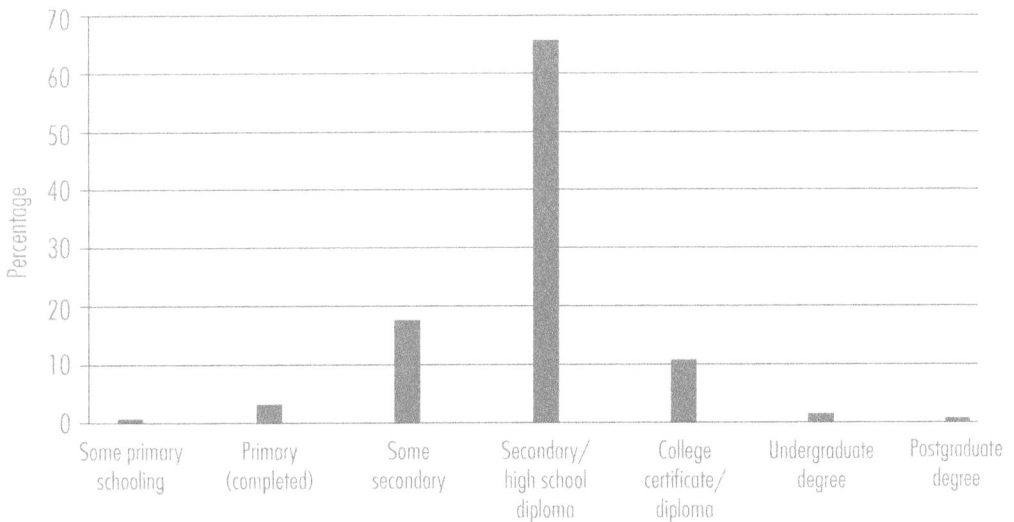

There is a common belief that cross-border trading is mostly for people who are single and free of commitments. However, only 17% of this sample had never married (Table 2). Two-thirds were married while 16% were divorced, separated or widowed. The largest number of traders were living in nuclear households (43%) (i.e. a household with a husband/male partner and wife/female partner with or without children), while 28% were from extended households (household with husband/male partner and wife/female partner and children and relatives) (Table 3). A significant minority of the traders (17%) were from female-centred (no husband/male partner) households while only 5% were male-centred.

The wide array of people involved in ICBT indicates that it is no longer the preserve of a few. An economic activity once dominated by low-income households and a relatively uneducated population has become a viable livelihood alternative for many others reeling under economic pressure. Although still dominated by women, male traders are involved in increasing numbers. Indeed, ICBT has become an occupation for all.

Table 2: Marital Status of ICBT Traders

	No.	%
Never married	91	17.2
Married/common law	351	66.5
Cohabiting	1	0.2
Divorced/separated	54	10.2
Widowed	31	5.9
Total	528	100.0

Table 3: Household Structure of ICBT Traders

	No.	%
Female-centred	97	18.3
Male-centred	26	4.9
Nuclear	228	42.9
Extended	145	27.3
Single-person household	35	6.6
Total	531	100.0

Only one percent of the ICBT businesses surveyed were established before 1990 (Table 4). This is primarily because the economy of the country was still strong at that time and most workers were being absorbed in the formal sector. Around 11% of the businesses were established in the 1990s, the decade of the Economic Structural Adjustment Programme (ESAP). Another 15% started cross-border trading between 2000 and 2005, but by far the largest proportion of ICBT traders began operations during and after the economic crisis of 2008, with nearly three-quarters starting up between 2006 and 2014. Interestingly, the rate of start-up seems to have fallen slightly after 2010. This may be a result of the stabilization of the economy as well as a more stable political environment. Because most food became available in the country through formal sector imports, the incentive to continue ICBT trade in foodstuffs was no longer so compelling. Moreover, the introduction of punitive duties on imported goods by the government meant that it mostly became cheaper to buy food and goods in the country than to import through the informal system.

Table 4: Year ICBT Business Was Established

	No.	%
Pre-1990	5	1.0
1991-1995	11	2.1
1996-2000	44	8.2
2001-2005	82	15.3
2006-2010	225	42.1
2011-2014	167	31.3
Total	534	100.0

Because high rates of unemployment are thought to be significant in pushing people into the informal economy and ICBT, the survey sought to find out what occupation the traders were engaged in prior to starting their enterprise. Around one-third were unemployed before starting their ICBT business (Table 5). Another 22% were already working in the informal economy, either running a business that did not involve ICBT or employed by someone else (6%). This suggests that the majority of traders went straight into ICBT, rather than expanding into ICBT from an existing enterprise. Another 36% of the traders were employed in a formal sector job immediately prior to establishing an ICBT business.

Around 30% of the sample indicated that they had additional sources of income while 70% relied solely on the ICBT business. The majority of those with alternative income-generating sources indicated that they were involved in another informal business, while 11% were deriving income from part-time or casual work (Table 6). According to one trader, having more than one business was a necessity given the unpredictable nature of informal trade:

> I sell clothes and shoes, but I also have another income from selling foodstuffs. Clothes do not sell faster than food so when I am in need of faster cash I know that I will always get some from trading food. However, the profit from food is not much so it just takes care of my immediate needs. When I am looking for serious money, I know I will get it from clothes and shoes even if they are bought less frequently.

Table 5: Occupation Before Starting ICBT Business

	No.	%
Unemployed		
Unemployed/job seeker	178	33.4
Informal economy		
Operated own informal sector business in Zimbabwe only	89	16.7
Employed by someone in the informal economy	32	6.0
Employed		
Office worker	40	7.5
Manual worker (skilled)	35	6.6
Manual worker (unskilled)	35	6.6
Professional (e.g. lawyer, doctor, academic, engineer)	15	2.8
Teacher	10	1.9
Health worker	9	1.7
Employer/manager	6	1.1
Police/military/security	4	0.8
Domestic worker	3	0.6
Agricultural worker	2	0.4
Other occupation	32	6.0
Other		
Business executive formal sector (self-employed)	7	1.3
Scholar/student	36	6.8
Total	533	100.0

Table 6: Other Income-Generating Activities

	No.	%
Another non-ICBT business	85	55.9
Part-time/casual work	17	11.2
Another ICBT business	14	9.2
Formal employment in the private sector	7	4.6
Formal employment in the public sector	3	2.0
Rentals	3	2.0
Other work	23	15.1
Total	152	100.0

ENTREPRENEURIAL MOTIVATION

There is an assumption in the literature on the informal economy in Zimbabwe that people participate because they have no choice. This would imply that most participants in ICBT are necessity-driven entrepreneurs, pushed rather than pulled to participate by the need to survive. However, ICBT is not the easiest or most obvious form of informal activity and may attract those with different, more opportunity-driven entrepreneurial motivations. The study therefore examined the reasons why traders started an ICBT business. Push factors that drive entrepreneurship relate mostly to employment factors. Pull factors include monetary or financial rewards; the desire for prestige, independence and intrinsic rewards (such as self-fulfilment and growth); and a desire to build human, social and financial capital.

Respondents were asked to rate 27 factors as motivations for starting an ICBT business on a scale from 1 (no importance) to 5 (extremely important). The responses certainly demonstrate the importance of financial survival in pushing people into cross-border trading (Table 7). Easily the most important factors were the need to make more money just to survive (a mean score of 4.9) and the need to give their family greater financial security (4.6). Generating employment for other family members was relatively unimportant. These findings suggest that ICBT is largely a necessity-driven survival strategy to generate income. Employment-related factors, including unemployment and having an undesirable job, were significantly less important.

The second set of factors relate more to self-assessment of personality traits usually associated with entrepreneurship. A desire to own one's own business did rate relatively highly (at 4.2), as did the related desire to be one's own boss (3.9). However, the other personality-related factors had low ratings, which suggests that the traders did not see themselves as natural entrepreneurs. However, they were alert to the market opportunities provided by participation in ICBT, with a number of factors scoring around 3.0 on average including awareness of shortages in Zimbabwe, having a good idea for a product to sell, and wanting to expand an existing business. Finally, the desire to take advantage of and build social capital with others were relatively unimportant motivational factors for entering ICBT.

Table 7: Entrepreneurial Motivation

Factor	Mean Score
Survivalist factors	
I needed more money just to survive	4.9
I wanted to give my family greater financial security	4.6
I was unemployed and unable to find a job	3.0
I had a job but it did not pay enough	2.6
I wanted to provide employment for members of my family	2.3
I had a job but it did not suit my qualifications and experience	1.2
Entrepreneurial orientation	
I have always wanted to run my own business	4.2
I wanted more control over my own time/to be my own boss	3.9
I like to challenge myself	2.9
I wanted to do something new and challenging	2.7
I have the right personality to be involved in cross-border trade	2.6
I wanted to compete with others and be the best	2.5
I like to learn new skills	2.5
I enjoy taking risks	2.4
Market opportunities	
I wanted to expand my business	3.2
I had a good idea for a product to sell to people in Zimbabwe	3.1
I started cross-border trading to grow my business	3.1
There were shortages of certain goods in my home country	3.0
I had a good idea for a product to sell in South Africa	1.2
I had a good idea for a product to sell to people from my home country in South Africa	1.2
Building and utilizing social capital	
I wanted to increase my status in the community	3.2
I wanted to contribute to the development of my home country	2.7
Support and help in starting my business was available from family members	2.5
I wanted to provide employment for other people	2.1
My family members have always been involved in cross-border trade	2.1
Support and help in starting my business was available from other traders	1.9
I decided to go into business in partnership with others	1.5

FINANCING THE ICBT ENTERPRISE

This section of the report deals with issues relating to the financing of ICBT businesses, including their source of start-up capital and ongoing loans. The amount of start-up capital required to engage in ICBT has been a deterrent for low-income individuals and households in the past.[14] In this survey, almost three-quarters of the sample had minimal start-up capital of ZAR5,000 or less, which suggests that the entry threshold may have declined (Figure 2). Only 8% had started their business with a capital outlay of more than ZAR10,000. According to some respondents, a basic ICBT business can be established with as little as ZAR2,000. As one trader observed:

> Cross-border business does not need a lot of money to start. You only need to be clever and buy things that sell faster and are wanted by the people. Then you can increase your stock as time goes on. I started my business with ZAR1,500 buying and selling rice when the country was in dire need of food. I would buy rice from Musina and sell in Harare and do two trips a week. I used trucks which are cheaper and did not sleep in South Africa, so I reduced my costs. I would carry my own food and use money only when necessary. Today, eight years later, my stock is worth over ZAR50,000. And my business is doing well. Now I buy from Johannesburg and can buy goods worth ZAR20,000 per single trip.

Figure 2: Capital Used to Start an ICBT Business

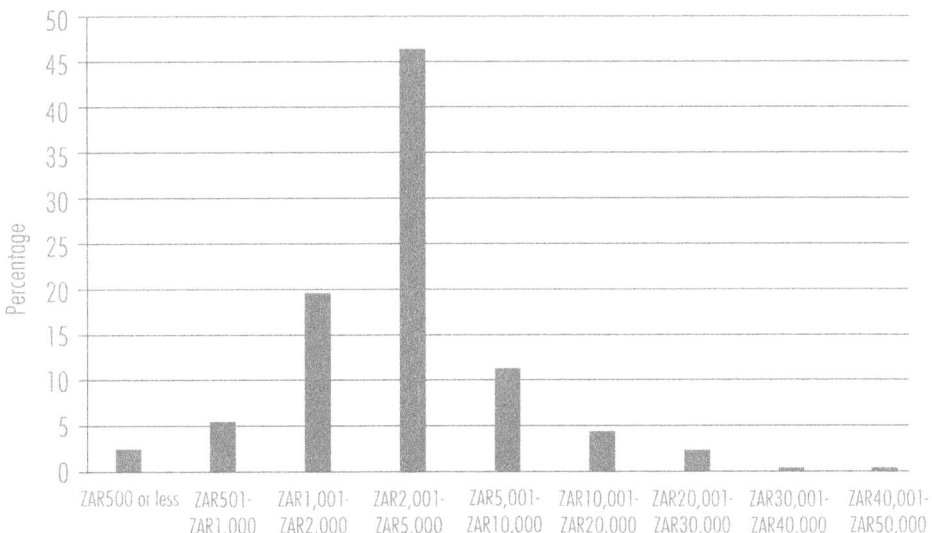

Most of the traders acquired their start-up capital from personal sources. Nearly 60% used their personal savings and another 38% borrowed money from relatives to get going (Table 8). Very few started their ICBT business with money from either informal sources (such as loans from non-relatives, informal financial institutions and money lenders) or from formal sources (such as banks and micro-finance institutions).

Table 8: Main Sources of Start-Up Capital for ICBT Business

	No.	%
Personal savings	311	58.0
Loan from relatives	203	38.0
Loan from non-relatives	9	1.7
Loan from informal financial institutions	7	1.3
Informal money lenders	5	0.9
Bank loan	4	0.8
Loan from micro-finance institution	2	0.4
Business credit (goods on terms)	1	0.2
Other source	63	12.0
N = 534		
Note: Multiple response question		

Almost one-third (27%) of the traders reported borrowing additional money for their business in the year prior to the study (Table 9). The majority of these had borrowed from relatives. According to the traders, relatives are the best source of loans because they do not place stringent conditions on the borrower and are likely to be understanding should they default on the loan or delay the repayment:

> Of course I have borrowed a number of times to finance my business, but I only borrow from my close relatives. They are very understanding when you can't pay them back or delay the repayment. If you borrow from other people, they give you all sorts of problems in that they can even come and take your goods as surety, or even sell your goods. Your relative, however, cannot just sell your goods or property over a debt. No, they cannot. They understand because we are of the same blood. My problems are their problems as well. So we always talk and agree on extending the repayment period or even cancellation of the entire debt.

Table 9: Sources of Operating Loans

	No.	%
Loan from relatives	77	53.0
Micro-finance institution	21	15.0
Bank	17	12.0
Informal financial institution	9	6.3
Money lenders	9	6.3
Loan from other business owners	6	4.2
Business credit (goods on terms)	1	0.7
Other sources	9	6.3
N = 144		
Note: Multiple response question		

Besides relatives, a small number had obtained their loans from micro-finance institutions (15%) and banks (12%). With the introduction of the United States dollar as the main trading currency in the country in 2009, a number of micro-finance institutions were established in Harare. These organizations lend money on a short-term basis, ranging from days to months, but rarely for periods exceeding one year. Their interest rates are generally higher than those offered by banks but they are less stringent on surety requirements. According to the traders, they will accept surety in the form of movable property (such as cars, fridges, stoves, televisions and washing machines). Banks, on the other hand, generally prefer immovable properties such as houses. In the absence of such property, a borrower is expected to show evidence of employment and ability to repay through submitting pay-slips. One trader compared the two in this way:

> I borrow many times when my stocks are low and I need to boost my business. I usually borrow from micro-finance houses where I can just leave the registration book of my car and get it when I repay them. I do not even have to take the car there. They just verify with their people at the vehicle registry department that indeed I own the car and that's it. With banks, they require a lot of documents and payslips which I do not have. I also do not own a house or stand to be used as surety. So I prefer the microfinances as they are simple. I can apply in the morning and get the money before the end of the day. With the banks, it may be a month before they tell you the outcome and I cannot wait that long.

Other sources of loans include informal financial institutions and money lenders. *Stokvels* (money clubs) lend money to members at reasonable rates and the repayment period is usually mutually agreed on with the borrower who is also a member. Hence, *stokvels* can be an attractive source for those who are members (30% of those interviewed). Money lenders, however, tend to lend at punitive rates and borrowers can end up repaying twice what they borrow. If the borrower has problems paying back the money, money lenders sometimes coerce repayment. Most ICBT traders thus stay away from them.

A few traders said they preferred to borrow from each other before going to banks and money lenders. This is because the terms of repayment from fellow traders are very favourable and there is a mutual understanding of the challenges of the trade. As one trader pointed out:

> *If my fellow trader has money to lend me, then that will be my first preference. This is because we understand each other and thus are unlikely to be cruel to one another. When one is late in repaying, we generally understand and do not harass each other, except when you can see that one is trying to deliberately take advantage of you. Then you can get rough with them and other people will understand your actions.*

Those who borrow from fellow traders average loans of ZAR16,667 compared to smaller amounts from banks (ZAR12,187), micro-finance institutions (ZAR11,214), informal financial institutions (ZAR7,444), relatives (ZAR6,335) and money lenders (ZAR3,527). One of the key factors determining from where money is borrowed is the interest charged on the loan. The highest interest rates are charged by money lenders (averaging 23%). Rates on loans from *stokvels* are surprisingly high (18%) compared to micro-finance institutions (17%) and banks (12%).

Loans from relatives attract the lowest interest rates, averaging only 4%. Some come interest-free and are viewed more as personal transactions:

> *I have never been charged any interest at all. These are my relatives and they are not aiming to profit from me. When my business does well, they also benefit because I bring them goods and food from my cross-border trading activities. Sometimes they ask me to buy them electrical gadgets and I do not put a mark-up on the price that I sell to them. I just sell to them at the same price that I buy the goods in Johannesburg. So, when I borrow from them, it is understood that they do not charge interest. We are family and we look after one another.*

Almost all of those borrowing money used the loans for the basic business activity of purchasing goods for resale (Table 10). Others used the funds to meet transportation costs. Most ICBT traders use public transport (buses and haulage trucks) to ferry their goods from South Africa and incur significant costs. Traders who take arts and curio products to South Africa to sell use the money to transport their goods as far afield as Cape Town and Port Elizabeth:

> I sell curios to tourists in Cape Town. The curios include drums, mats, bowls, wood and stone carvings as well as other little paraphernalia. I usually spend two to three months buying these products and storing at home. So during that time I will not be making money as all the money will be locked in my stock. When I have accumulated many things, I then travel to Cape Town. By the time that I leave for Cape Town, I will have very little money, so I borrow from friends and relatives and give them back when I return. Sometimes I stay in Cape Town for one to two months, depending on how fast my stock is selling.

A few traders use their loans to rent stalls from which to sell their products. In Harare, some traders have no stalls of their own and rent from others on a daily, weekly or monthly basis.

Table 10: Use of Loans by ICBT Traders

	No.	%
Purchase of goods for sale	137	95.0
Transportation of goods from South Africa	43	30.0
Transportation to South Africa	39	27.0
Rental of market stall	15	10.0
Expansion of the business activity	5	3.3
Improvement of business premises	2	1.4
Acquisition or maintenance of equipment	1	0.7
Accommodation in South Africa	1	0.7
Repayment of previous debts	1	0.7
Other uses	8	5.6
N = 144		
Note: Multiple response question		

What is clear is that loans are used for basic business expenses and not for other household needs. Most traders indicated that the borrowed money significantly increased the volume of sales (Figure 3). Others reported an increase in the profitability and competitiveness of their business; diversification of the products that they traded; and a decrease in financial problems. However, not all had positive experiences:

> I borrowed ZAR20,000 from a micro-finance in March so that I could buy more stock. However, that loan has caused me more problems than any real benefits because from that time everything has been going downhill. The interest rate was such that I was expected to pay back the ZAR20,000 plus ZAR5,000 interest in two months. When I bought more stock from Johannesburg, I paid too much duty at the border and when I resold the goods in Harare, I failed to raise the initial ZAR20,000 and by the end of the two months I could only pay back ZAR14,000 instead of the ZAR25,000 that I owed. The micro-finance then took my car and gave me seven days to pay or risk the car being sold. I failed to raise the ZAR11,000 that was still outstanding and the car was sold. I used to sell my clothes and shoes from the back of my car and now I have nothing to conduct business with. I am ruined. I only wish I had not borrowed in the first place.

Figure 3: Impact of Loans on ICBT Business Activity

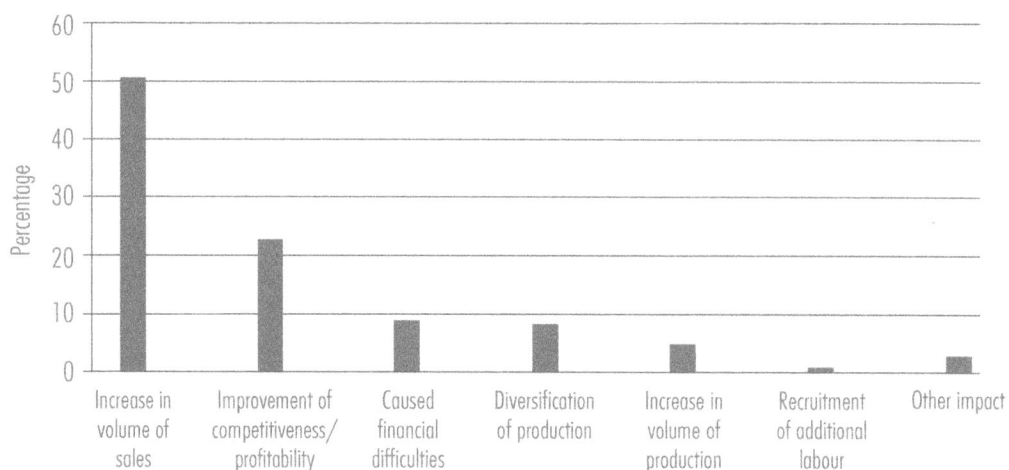

Less than 20% of the ICBT traders had applied for a bank loan to finance their business. Around one-quarter indicated that they had no interest in getting a loan from a bank but only 8% said that they had not applied for a loan because they had sufficient capital. Other reasons given included the high interest rates, complicated application procedures and the collateral demanded by the banks (Table 11). According to one trader:

> *I have seen a lot of people losing houses to banks because of these loans. Most of them were well-respected people, but now they are homeless and almost destitute. I do what I can with the money that I raise from my business and from friends. I will never approach a bank, they will just ruin me. So far, I have been doing well on my own and have no need to change that by inviting them to share in my business.*

Table 11: Main Reason for Not Applying for a Bank Loan

	No.	%
I am not interested in getting a loan	101	24.5
Guarantee/collateral asked for is too much	59	14.3
Interest rates are too high	54	13.1
Application procedures are too complicated	49	11.9
Did not think it would be approved	47	11.4
I don't have a bank account	46	11.2
No need for a loan — establishment has sufficient capital	33	8.0
Other reason	23	5.6
Total	412	100.0

Only half of those who had applied for a bank loan were successful. Most were rejected because they had insufficient collateral. According to a trader whose application had been rejected, the documentation required by the bank was onerous:

> *I have applied for a loan more than three times, and every time my application is rejected I am given a different reason. The first time I was told that I did not have sufficient collateral even though I had submitted title deeds for a plot that I bought with my wife. Because my wife is now living out of the country, they asked me to submit a letter from her assenting to the use of the deed, which she did. Then I was told that the letter was not sufficient but that I should also submit a power of attorney from her. The third time I was told that the amount of money I needed was too much and could not be covered by the plot. I eventually*

just gave up. But it is frustrating after having wasted so much time and money looking for documents, printing and posting documents from out of the country and travelling to and from the bank.

TRAVELLING TO JOHANNESBURG

The ICBT traders are highly mobile, spending only 1.8 days in South Africa on average per visit, although some stay for several weeks, particularly if they are taking goods to sell. The traders travel relatively frequently to South Africa, with 67% making at least one trip per month and 82% travelling more than four times per year. The vast majority do not have their own means of transport to South Africa and rely on bus services (Table 12). Important in the informal movement of goods and remittances between migrants in South Africa and family in Zimbabwe are transport operators commonly known as *omalayisha*.[15] However, some ICBT traders also use their services to avoid having to transport their own goods through the border. The *omalayisha* are well-known to the customs officials on both sides of the border, which enables them to carry goods without paying customs duties.

Table 12: Main Mode of Transportation Used to Travel to Johannesburg

	No.	%
Bus	530	99.0
Trucks	21	3.9
Own vehicle	6	1.1
Taxi	3	0.6
Rent vehicle with friends/rent space in vehicle	1	0.2
Aeroplane	1	0.2
N = 534		
Note: Multiple response question		

In Johannesburg, the majority of traders purchase their goods at a small number of outlets, especially China Mall (26%), other Chinese-run malls (25%) and Oriental Plaza (5%) (Figure 4).[16] Some buy their goods from wholesalers (14%), while others patronize independent small shops/retailers (13%) or small shops/retailers in malls (8%). A much smaller number purchase goods from factories, supermarkets, the informal sector and directly from farmers.

Figure 4: Source of Goods in Johannesburg

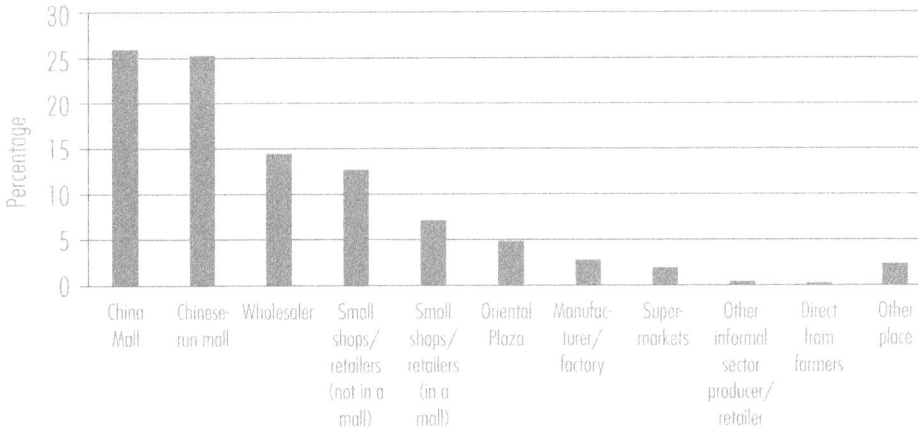

There are probably many ICBT traders in Harare who do not travel as far as Johannesburg, preferring instead to shop at South African border towns such as Musina. However, as many as 78% also buy goods from Musina en route to Zimbabwe from Johannesburg. Another important finding was that these cross-border traders also buy goods in other countries. As many as 72% buy goods from countries including Botswana (40%), Zambia (32%), Mozambique (11%) and Tanzania (10%).

The kinds of goods purchased in South Africa for resale in Zimbabwe vary widely (Table 13). By far the most common items are new clothing and shoes, with 88% of all traders buying these items. Other goods include accessories such as bags and suitcases (bought by 27%), bedding materials (20%), electronics (12%) and household products (8%). Foodstuffs, which were carried by three-quarters of ICBT traders in 2008, were not at all popular with the traders in 2014.[17] This is a reflection of post-2009 developments in Zimbabwe that led to a more abundant supply of food products in the country.[18] On a typical trip, the traders spend an average of ZAR8,328 on a variety of products for resale, with a minimum of ZAR1,000 and a maximum of ZAR150,000.

Table 13: Goods Bought in South Africa

	No.	%
New clothing and footwear	467	87.6
Accessories (bags, sunglasses etc.)	141	26.4
Bedding	104	19.5
Electronics	64	12.0
Household products	41	7.7
Hardware/tools	31	5.8
Toiletries and cosmetics	30	5.6
Cellphones/accessories	24	4.5
CDs/DVDs	15	3.5
Cooking oil	11	2.1
Second-hand clothing and footwear	9	1.7
Furniture	5	0.9
Stationery	5	0.9
Rice and pasta	4	0.8
Tea/coffee	4	0.8
Sugar	4	0.8
Beds and mattresses	4	0.8
Milk (fresh/sour)	3	0.6
Spare parts and raw materials	2	0.4
Eggs	2	0.4
Snacks	2	0.4
Car parts	2	0.4
Confectionary	1	0.2
Mealie meal	1	0.2
Bread	1	0.2
Tinned/canned fruits and vegetables	1	0.2
Plastic goods	1	0.2
Toys, sports equipment	1	0.2
N = 533		
Note: Multiple response question		

Only a few traders said that they take products from Zimbabwe to sell in South Africa. The main products include arts and crafts, fabrics, bedding, household products and new clothes and shoes.

SELLING GOODS IN ZIMBABWE

Although the overwhelming majority of the traders sell their goods in the country's capital, where the survey was conducted, more than 10% also sell goods in other major cities such as Bulawayo and Masvingo and in smaller urban centres such as Gokwe and Mutoko. As many as 86% of the traders sell their products in their own stall in an informal market while 24% sell through friends, family and other personal networks (Table 14). A further 16% sell their products from their own house, 10% from their own shop in the informal sector and 9% on the street. Door-to-door sales are conducted by 7% of the respondents.

Table 14: Location Where Goods are Sold in Harare

	No.	%
Own stall in informal market	460	86.3
Friends/family/networks	128	24.0
From my house	87	16.3
Own shop in informal sector	51	9.6
On the street	48	9.0
Door to door	36	6.8
Sellers in informal markets	16	3.0
Other offices/workplaces	13	2.4
Rural areas	8	1.5
Own shop in formal sector	8	1.5
Mines and farms	4	0.8
Retailers and shops	4	0.8
Own office/workplace	1	0.2
Wholesalers	1	0.2
N = 533		
Note: Multiple response question		

CONTRIBUTIONS TO THE ZIMBABWEAN ECONOMY

An important objective of this research was to assess the importance of ICBT trade to the economies of both Zimbabwe and South Africa. This is particularly important in the case of Zimbabwe where the informal economy is viewed by government as a problem and a hindrance to the success of formal businesses. First, it is clear from the wide variety of goods imported by the ICBT traders that there is a ready market in Zimbabwe for their products. This means that the traders are servicing the needs of Zimbabwean consumers either by providing cheaper goods or goods that would otherwise be unavailable in the country. Given the high rates of unemployment and the fact that many households are cash-strapped, the ICBT traders play a critical role in servicing the basic consumer needs of Zimbabweans.

Second, the ICBT enterprises contribute to the economy through business establishment, growth and the strategic deployment of their profits. On average, the surveyed traders were recording total sales worth ZAR12,000 per month. Sales ranged from as low as ZAR1,000 per month for the small traders to as high as ZAR130,000 per month for those dealing in large quantities of goods, especially those trading in hardware and building materials. The reported profits averaged ZAR4,765 per month but were highly variable, ranging from a minimum of ZAR200 per month to a maximum of ZAR45,000 per month. Traders with high sales turnover generally reported higher monthly profits. These profits indicate that ICBT is not just a survivalist enterprise and that sizable gains can be made. More than half (59%) of the ICBT operators reported that their income had increased since embarking on ICBT (Table 15). A further 24% reported that their income was variable, sometimes increasing and at other times decreasing. Only 15% indicated that their income had decreased since starting an ICBT business.

Table 15: Impact of ICBT on Income

	No.	%
My income has increased	309	58.5
My income has not changed/remained the same	17	3.2
My income has decreased	78	14.8
Variable	124	23.5
Total	528	100.0

Third, given that the income of the majority of the traders had improved significantly through ICBT, it is important to know whether they use their profits for the business itself or outside the business. Almost one-third (32%) reported spending their profits on family needs, including paying rent for accommodation, buying food for the family and other obligatory family expenses (Table 16). Another 15% used their profits for education, such as school fees for dependants, and 14% spent the funds on themselves. Only one-quarter reinvest their profits in the business, which suggests that the demands of family and household may constrain business expansion. Again, only 10% are able to save any of their profits.

Table 16: Use of Business Profits

	No.	%
Spent on family needs (in home country)	489	32.1
Re-investment in business in home country	391	25.7
Education	230	15.1
Spent on myself	210	13.8
Personal savings	152	10.0
Spent on family needs (outside home country — remittances)	3	0.2
Retirement fund	3	0.2
Re-investment in business outside home country	4	0.3
Other	39	2.6
Total	1,521	100.0

Note: Multiple response question

Fourth, as well as stimulating the economy through the reinvestment of profits inside and outside the business, the ICBT traders contribute to Zimbabwe's economy through job creation. Most traders focus on procuring goods themselves in South Africa and hire people to sell the goods in Zimbabwe. A total of 37% of the traders employ people in Zimbabwe as part of their business:

- Of the 308 people employed, 236 (or 77%) were in paid positions (Table 17 and Figure 5).

- Even when members of the family are involved in the business, they tend to be compensated for their time. Of the 128 family members employed, 71% were in paid positions.

- As many as 61% of the paid jobs went to non-family members.

- Of the 236 paid employees, only 28% were men. Participation in the businesses set up by the traders is thus heavily female-oriented.

In sum, employment generated by the cross-border traders is shared fairly evenly between family and non-family members and there is a general preference for female labour in the business hires. Around 10% of the traders involve their children in their business activities, either in selling goods (59%) or looking after a stall (40%).

Table 17: Employment Creation by ICBT Traders

	No. of employees	Family members (>18 years)		Family members (<18 years)		Non-family employees	
		No.	%	No.	%	No.	%
Paid – Male	1	11	4.7	8	3.4	25	10.6
	2	2	0.8	2	0.8	3	1.3
	3	0	0.0	0	0.0	1	0.4
	4	0	0.0	0	0.0	1	0.4
Paid – Female	1	25	10.6	13	5.5	50	21.2
	2	3	1.3	5	2.1	17	7.2
	3	1	0.4	1	0.4	2	0.8
	4	0	0.0	1	0.4	4	1.7
Unpaid – Male	1	5	2.1	3	1.3	1	0.4
	2	2	0.8	0	0.0	1	0.4
	3	1	0.4	0	0.0	0	0.0
Unpaid – Female	1	18	7.6	14	5.9	3	1.3
	2	5	2.1	4	1.7	2	0.8
	3	0	0.0	0	0.0	1	0.4

Finally, other beneficiaries include the Zimbabwean bus companies and the general Zimbabwean fiscus, which benefits from duties levied at the border on returning traders bringing in products with a value above the duty-free limit. On their last trip to South Africa, the ICBT traders paid ZAR431 on average in customs duties, which amounts to ZAR228,529 levied on these traders alone. Given that this sample is only a small proportion of the total number of ICBT traders, the total levied undoubtedly runs into millions of rands.

Figure 5: Total Number of People Employed in ICBT Businesses

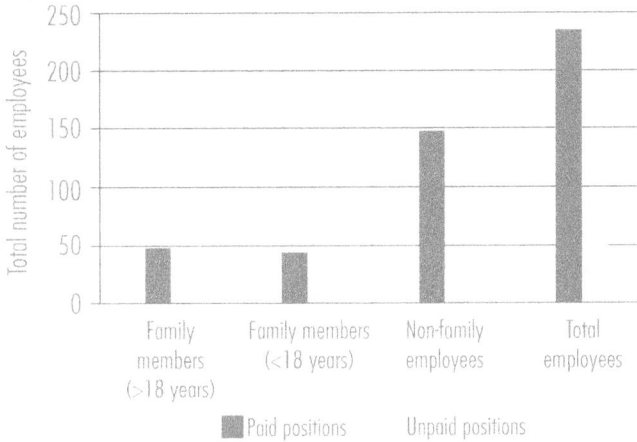

CONTRIBUTIONS TO THE SOUTH AFRICAN ECONOMY

First, the ICBT traders contribute to the South African economy through various expenditures while in the country (Figure 6). Clearly, the largest beneficiaries are the South African wholesalers from whom the traders purchase their goods. The traders also support the South African transport and hospitality industries. Overall, they spent an average of ZAR8,039 on their last trip to South Africa. The spend on particular items included ZAR6,737 on goods (or ZAR3.5 million in total), ZAR683 on transportation (ZAR361,000 in total), ZAR42 on accommodation (ZAR22,000 in total) and R141 on other costs.

Figure 6: Amounts Spent on Last Trip to South Africa

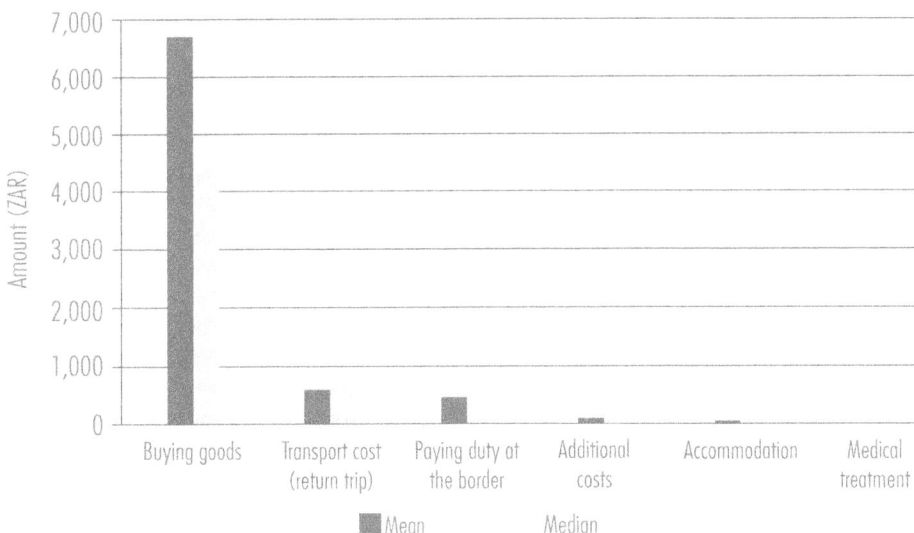

Second, South Africa benefits from the VAT paid by the traders. Visitors to South Africa who buy goods for use in their home country are eligible to apply for a VAT refund when they exit the country. When they buy goods in South Africa, visitors should request a tax invoice containing the following information:

- The words "tax invoice";

- The seller's name and address;

- The seller's 10-digit VAT registration number;

- The date of issue of the tax invoice;

- A tax invoice number;

- A full description of the goods purchased with second-hand goods indicated as such;

- The cost of the goods supplied in rands;

- The amount of VAT charged, or a statement that VAT at the rate of 14% is included in the total cost of the goods; and

- In the case of purchases over ZAR5,000, the purchaser's name and physical address and the quantity or volume of the goods must appear on the tax invoice.

However, only 22% of the cross-border traders reported that they claimed VAT back at the border (Table 18). Over one-third (37%) did not know that they could claim VAT refunds at the border. Another third said that the process of claiming VAT at the border takes too long. This is exacerbated by the fact that ownership levels of motor vehicles are very low and reliance on public transport is high, which means that they have limited time to wait. Nearly 10% noted that the receipts provided by South African retailers are invalid for the purpose of claiming VAT refunds. Receipts from Chinese-owned shops, in particular, do not meet the requirements for refunds. Others do not claim VAT refunds because they do not want to declare their goods and feel that claiming exposes their goods to customs scrutiny. Clearly, there is insufficient information available on the procedures for claiming VAT refunds at the border.

Table 18: Reason for Not Claiming VAT Refunds at the Border

	No.	%
Did not know that I can claim VAT at the border	154	36.9
Process takes too long	136	32.6
Receipts are invalid	41	9.8
Goods are smuggled	31	7.4
Goods not eligible for VAT	24	5.8
Cannot cash cheque	17	4.1
Receipts are given to *amalayisha* transporters	10	2.4
Other reason	4	1.0
Total	417	100.0

BUSINESS PROBLEMS AND CHALLENGES

Cross-border traders confront numerous challenges in the course of their business activities. These are of two main types: (a) those related to customs and immigration at the border and (b) those related to their daily business operations in both South Africa and Zimbabwe.

CUSTOMS AND IMMIGRATION

In terms, first, of customs or immigration-related problems experienced at the border, by far the most common problems relate to the queues and delays, experienced often by 74% and sometimes by 23% of the respondents (Table 19). ICBT has become a way of life for a significant number of Zimbabweans and this has put pressure on immigration officials at Beitbridge and Musina border posts. Consequently, long delays at the border post are legion. Another common problem experienced by the traders relates to the high duties levied at the border (60% said that they often experience this problem). In his mid-term fiscal policy review statement in September 2014, Zimbabwean Finance Minister Patrick China-masa increased duty on various finished products including meat and dairy products, beverages, vegetables, soap and furniture.[19] He also removed foodstuffs, beverages and washing preparations from the duty-free facility. While the stated rationale for these measures was to protect local industry, the local companies that had produced these goods closed at the height of the economic crisis in 2007-2008. Consequently, imposing higher duties does not deter traders from bringing these goods into the country, but simply burdens the general population who rely on these goods from the traders.

Table 19: Problems Experienced at Borders

	Often	Some-times	Never
	%	%	%
Long queues/congestion/delays at border post	73.7	22.7	3.6
Duties paid are too high	60.4	25.1	14.4
Restrictions on import/export of goods (type and volume)	45.5	32.1	22.5
Too much corruption at border post	38.8	28.0	33.1
Transport problems/poor road networks/transport prices high	29.6	42.5	27.9
Verbal harassment by South African police, army, border officials	15.0	21.2	63.7
Unwarranted confiscation/detention of goods	11.4	30.2	58.3
Days allowed in South Africa are too few	10.4	15.8	73.8
Physical harassment/assault by South African police, army, border officials	5.6	12.4	81.9
Verbal harassment by police, army, border officials of Zimbabwe	4.0	14.9	81.2
Physical harassment/assault by other people	2.3	14.5	83.2
Physical harassment/assault by Zimbabwean police, army, border officials	2.3	7.3	90.4

Other problems cited by a significant number of traders include restrictions on the import or export of goods (55% often), corruption (39% often) and verbal harassment by South African police, army, border officials (15% often). The problem of corruption has been highlighted elsewhere.[20] The delays at the border have created an opportunity for touts who know that the traders want to cross the border quickly and will pay a small fee for officials to speed up the clearing processes for them. Some traders have also lost money to bogus agents masquerading as immigration and customs officials.

While harassment, both verbal and physical, was highlighted as a problem by a small number of traders, the figures are high enough to be a cause for concern. For instance, verbal harassment by South African police, army and border officials was experienced often by 15% and sometimes by 21% of the respondents. In Zimbabwe, the incidence is lower with 4% experiencing such abuse often and 15% sometimes. As worrisome is the physical harassment/beating/violation of human rights by South African police, army and border officials that is experienced often by 6% and sometimes by 12% of the respondents. Thus, nearly one in five of the traders have been subjected to physical abuse by the South African police, army and border officials. On the Zimbabwean side of the border, such abuse is again lower at 9%.

BUSINESS COMPETITION

Perhaps the biggest business challenge confronting cross-border traders is competition from other traders (experienced often/sometimes by 84%) (Table 20). Another significant problem is the competition from large retailers or supermarkets (experienced often/sometimes by 60%). These outlets enjoy economies of scale as they buy goods in bulk from suppliers at low prices and are able to price their goods competitively. However, even the large supermarkets cannot outdo the informal sector traders. For instance, beverages, foodstuffs and detergents are sold on pavements in Harare at cheaper prices than those charged by supermarkets.

Given the evidence of pervasive animosity of South African informal entrepreneurs towards foreign-owned enterprises, it is notable that few of the ICBT traders from Zimbabwe experience serious problems: only 8% often/sometimes experience harassment by South African competitors.[21] Harassment by the South African municipal authorities is only marginally more common (13%). However, as many as 39% had often/sometimes experienced this form of harassment in Harare. This is consistent with the findings of recent studies on the difficulties faced by informal street traders in the city.[22] Other significant problems experienced by the traders in their daily operations include theft of money or goods (47% often/sometimes), confiscation of goods and difficulty getting merchandise back thereafter (25%), and discrimination based on gender and nationality.

A related dimension of discrimination is the challenge posed by xenophobia in South Africa. As many as 78% have not been affected by xenophobia at all in their business operations, while only 4% have been affected a great deal and 8% to some extent. Almost an equal number (30% and 28% in Zimbabwe and South Africa respectively) have been robbed, which indicates that the traders are at risk of crime in both Zimbabwe and South Africa, primarily because their business is cash-based. In June 2016, for example, there were reports of a spate of robberies in South Africa targeting buses carrying cross-border traders from Zimbabwe, bringing to the fore the dangers that traders face.[23]

Table 20: Problems Related to Business Operations

	Often	Sometimes	Never
	%	%	%
Business competition			
Competition from other traders	51.9	32.1	16.0
Competition from large retailers or supermarkets	20.5	39.5	39.9
Difficulty negotiating with other traders/conflicts among traders	10.6	39.1	50.4
Harassment by South African traders	1.9	6.5	91.6
Operational challenges			
Insecurity of selling site and/or problems securing a selling site when needed in Zimbabwe	13.1	16.1	70.7
No relevant training in accounting, marketing, other business skills	7.4	23.1	69.5
Theft of money or goods	7.3	39.5	53.1
Policy environment			
Harassment by authorities in Zimbabwe (e.g. police or other officials)	13.0	26.4	60.6
Harassment by authorities in South Africa (e.g. police or other officials)	2.8	10.0	87.2
Confiscation of goods/difficulty getting merchandise back after confiscation	5.3	19.8	74.9
Discrimination			
Prejudice against my nationality	11.8	24.8	63.4
Prejudice against my gender	3.2	13.3	83.5

CONCLUSION

This report has provided detailed insights into the current activities of cross-border traders from Harare who travel to Johannesburg as part of their business. The traders travel regularly to South Africa (three-quarters go at least once per month) and make a monthly profit of more than ZAR4,000 per month, which exceeds the salaries of most people in formal employment. This is despite a small initial capital outlay, averaging around ZAR5,000 for the initial investment. Furthermore, the traders have been able to grow their businesses to such an extent that they hire people from outside their families. ICBT has become more than a survivalist strategy and should be seen as an important pillar of the Zimbabwean economy. The contribution of the informal economy in generating jobs and reducing unemployment needs to be acknowledged by policies that encourage rather than restrict the operation of informal trade.

ENDNOTES

1   "Zimbabwe Bans a Host of Goods from Being Imported" *Pindula News* 19 June 2016.

2   Scoones, "Zimbabwe's Riots"; Kalaba, "Lessons to be Learnt."

3   Finmark Trust, *FinScope MSME Survey*.

4   Mijere, *Informal Cross-Border Trade in the Southern African Development Community*; Makombe, "Informal Cross-Border Trade and SADC"; Peberdy et al. "Transnational Entrepreneurship and Informal Cross-Border Trade with South Africa."

5   Muzvidziwa, "Cross-Border Trade."

6   Gaidzanwa, "Cross-Border Trade in Southern Africa"; Muzvidziwa, "Cross-Border Women Traders."

7   Potts, "'Restoring Order'?"; Chirisa, "Post-2005 Harare"; Kamete, "Not Exactly Like the Phoenix."

8   Tevera and Tawodzera, "Cross-Border Trade."

9   Kachere, "Informal Cross Border Trading and Poverty Reduction"; Ama et al. "Profitability of the Informal Cross-Border Trade"; Campbell and Crush, "They Don't Want Foreigners."

10 Tawodzera, "Household Food Insecurity and Survival in Harare."

11 Muzvidziwa, "Gendered Nature of Informal Crossborder Trade in Zimbabwe."

12 UNIFEM, *Women in Informal Cross Border Trade in Southern Africa*.

13 Muzvidziwa, "Cross-Border Women Traders."

14 Muzvidziwa, *Women Without Borders*.

15 Thebe, "Malayisha Industry and the Transnational Movement of Remittances."

16 See Laribee, "The China Shop Phenomenon."

17 Peberdy et al., "Transnational Entrepreneurship and Informal Cross-Border Trade."

18 Tawodzera, "Household Food Insecurity and Survival in Harare."

19 Rusvingo, "Chinamasa's Mid-Term Fiscal Policy Review Statement."

20 Fitzmaurice, "Situational Analysis at Beitbridge Border Post"; Kwanisai et al., "Borders as Barriers to Tourism."

21 Crush and Ramachandran, "Doing Business With Xenophobia."

22 Njaya, "Challenges of Negotiating Sectoral Governance"; Njaya, "Coping with Informality and Illegality"; Rogerson, "Responding to Informality in Urban Africa."

23 "South Africa: Eagle Liner Bus Robbed, Burnt in South Africa" *The Herald* 21 June 2016; "Another Zim Bus Robbed in SA" *The Chronicle* 25 June 2016.

REFERENCES

1. Ama, N., Mangadi, K., Okurut, F. and Ama, H. (2013). "Profitability of the Informal Cross-Border Trade: A Case Study of Four Selected Borders in Botswana" *African Journal of Business Management* 7: 4221-32.

2. Campbell, E. and Crush, J. (2014). "They Don't Want Foreigners: Zimbabwean Migration and Xenophobia in Botswana" *Crossings: Journal of Migration and Culture* 6: 159-80.

3. Chirisa, I. (2007). "Post-2005 Harare: A Case of the Informal Sector and Street Vending Resilience: What Options Do Key Actors Have?" *Local Governance and Development Journal* 1: 53-64.

4. Crush, J. and Ramachandran, S. (2015). "Doing Business With Xenophobia" In J. Crush, A. Chikanda and C. Skinner (eds.), *Mean Streets: Migration, Xenophobia and Informality in South Africa* (Cape Town and Ottawa: SAMP and IDRC).

5. Finmark Trust (2014). *FinScope MSME Survey Zimbabwe 2012* (Harare).

6. Fitzmaurice, M. (2009). "Situational Analysis at Beitbridge Border Post between Zimbabwe and South Africa" Report by Transport Logistics Consultants.

7. Gaidzanwa, R. (1998). "Cross-Border Trade in Southern Africa: A Gendered Perspective" In L. Sachikonye (ed.) *Labour Markets and Migration Policy in Southern Africa* (Harare: SAPES Trust).

8. Kachere, W. (2011). "Informal Cross Border Trading and Poverty Reduction in the Southern African Development Community: The Case of Zimbabwe" PhD Thesis, University of Fort Hare, South Africa.

9. Kalaba, M. (2016). "Lessons to be Learnt from Zimbabwe's Blunt Use of an Import Ban" *The Conversation* 27 July.

10. Kamete, A. (2012). "Not Exactly Like the Phoenix – But Rising All the Same: Reconstructing Livelihoods in Post-Cleanup Harare" *Society and Space* 30: 243-61.

11. Kwanisai, G., Mpofu, T., Vengesayi, S., Mutanga, D., Hurombo, B. and Mirimi, K. (2014). "Borders as Barriers to Tourism: Tourists Experiences at the Beitbridge Border Post" *African Journal of Hospitality, Tourism and Leisure* 3: 1-13.

12. Laribee, R. (2008). "The China Shop Phenomenon: Trade Supply Within the Chinese Diaspora in South Africa" *Africa Spectrum* 13: 353–70.

13. Makombe, P. (2011). "Informal Cross-Border Trade and SADC: The Search for Greater Recognition" Open Society Initiative for Southern Africa, Johannesburg.

14. Mijere, N. (2009). *Informal Cross-Border Trade in the Southern African Development Community (SADC)* (Addis Ababa: OSSREA).

15. Muzvidziwa, V. (1998). "Cross-Border Trade: A Strategy for Climbing Out of Poverty in Masvingo, Zimbabwe" *Zambezia* 25: 29-58.

16. Muzvidziwa, V. (2001). "Cross-Border Women Traders: Multiple Identities and Responses to New Challenges" *Journal of Contemporary African Studies* 19: 67–80.

17. Muzvidziwa, V. (2007). *Women Without Borders: Informal Cross-Border Trade Among Women in the Southern African Development Community* (Addis Ababa: OSSREA).

18. Muzvidziwa, V. (2015). "Gendered Nature of Informal Crossborder Trade in Zimbabwe" *Journal of Social Development in Africa* 30: 131-46.

19. Njaya, T. (2014). "Challenges of Negotiating Sectoral Governance of Street Vending Sector in Harare Metropolitan, Zimbabwe" *Asian Journal of Economic Modelling* 2: 69-84.

20. Njaya, T. (2014). "Coping with Informality and Illegality: The Case of Street Entrepreneurs of Harare, Metropolitan Zimbabwe" *Asian Journal of Economic Modelling* 2: 93-102.

21. Peberdy, S., Crush, J., Tevera, D., Campbell, E., Zindela, N., Raimundo, I., Green, T., Chikanda, A. and Tawodzera, G. (2015). "Transnational Entrepreneurship and Informal Cross-Border Trade with South Africa" In J. Crush, A. Chikanda and C. Skinner (eds.) *Mean Streets: Migration, Xenophobia and Informality in South Africa* (Cape Town and Ottawa: SAMP and IDRC), pp. 207-28.

22. Potts, D. (2006). "'Restoring Order'? Operation Murambatsvina and the Urban Crisis in Zimbabwe" *Journal of Southern African Studies* 32: 273-91.

23. Rogerson, C. (2016). Responding to Informality in Urban Africa: Street Trading in Harare, Zimbabwe" *Urban Forum* 27: 229-51.

24. Rusvingo, S. (2014). "Chinamasa's Mid-Term Fiscal Policy Review Statement: A Dog's Breakfast" *Global Journal of Human-Social Science: (E) Economics* 14.

25. Scoones, I. (2016). "Zimbabwe's Riots: The Rise of the Informal Trader and a New Political Economy" *The Conversation* 14 July.

26. Tawodzera, G. (2015). "Household Food Insecurity and Survival in Harare: 2008 and Beyond" *Urban Forum* 25: 207-16.

27. Tevera, D. and Tawodzera, G. (2007). "Cross-Border Trade: The Case of Beitbridge, Forbes, Chirundu and Nyamapanda Border Posts" Report for SAMP, University of Zimbabwe, Harare.

28. Thebe, V. (2015). "The Malayisha Industry and the Transnational Movement of Remittances to Zimbabwe" In J. Crush, A. Chikanda and C. Skinner (eds.), *Mean Streets: Migration, Xenophobia and Informality in South Africa* (Cape Town and Ottawa: SAMP and IDRC), pp. 194-206.

29. UNIFEM (2010). *Women in Informal Cross Border Trade in Southern Africa* (Johannesburg: UNIFEM).

MIGRATION POLICY SERIES

1 *Covert Operations: Clandestine Migration, Temporary Work and Immigration Policy in South Africa* (1997) ISBN 1-874864-51-9

2 *Riding the Tiger: Lesotho Miners and Permanent Residence in South Africa* (1997) ISBN 1-874864-52-7

3 *International Migration, Immigrant Entrepreneurs and South Africa's Small Enterprise Economy* (1997) ISBN 1-874864-62-4

4 *Silenced by Nation Building: African Immigrants and Language Policy in the New South Africa* (1998) ISBN 1-874864-64-0

5 *Left Out in the Cold? Housing and Immigration in the New South Africa* (1998) ISBN 1-874864-68-3

6 *Trading Places: Cross-Border Traders and the South African Informal Sector* (1998) ISBN 1-874864-71-3

7 *Challenging Xenophobia: Myth and Realities about Cross-Border Migration in Southern Africa* (1998) ISBN 1-874864-70-5

8 *Sons of Mozambique: Mozambican Miners and Post-Apartheid South Africa* (1998) ISBN 1-874864-78-0

9 *Women on the Move: Gender and Cross-Border Migration to South Africa* (1998) ISBN 1-874864-82-9

10 *Namibians on South Africa: Attitudes Towards Cross-Border Migration and Immigration Policy* (1998) ISBN 1-874864-84-5

11 *Building Skills: Cross-Border Migrants and the South African Construction Industry* (1999) ISBN 1-874864-84-5

12 *Immigration & Education: International Students at South African Universities and Technikons* (1999) ISBN 1-874864-89-6

13 *The Lives and Times of African Immigrants in Post-Apartheid South Africa* (1999) ISBN 1-874864-91-8

14 *Still Waiting for the Barbarians: South African Attitudes to Immigrants and Immigration* (1999) ISBN 1-874864-91-8

15 *Undermining Labour: Migrancy and Sub-Contracting in the South African Gold Mining Industry* (1999) ISBN 1-874864-91-8

16 *Borderline Farming: Foreign Migrants in South African Commercial Agriculture* (2000) ISBN 1-874864-97-7

17 *Writing Xenophobia: Immigration and the Press in Post-Apartheid South Africa* (2000) ISBN 1-919798-01-3

18 *Losing Our Minds: Skills Migration and the South African Brain Drain* (2000) ISBN 1-919798-03-x

19 *Botswana: Migration Perspectives and Prospects* (2000) ISBN 1-919798-04-8

20 *The Brain Gain: Skilled Migrants and Immigration Policy in Post-Apartheid South Africa* (2000) ISBN 1-919798-14-5

21 *Cross-Border Raiding and Community Conflict in the Lesotho-South African Border Zone* (2001) ISBN 1-919798-16-1

22 *Immigration, Xenophobia and Human Rights in South Africa* (2001) ISBN 1-919798-30-7

23 *Gender and the Brain Drain from South Africa* (2001) ISBN 1-919798-35-8

24 *Spaces of Vulnerability: Migration and HIV/AIDS in South Africa* (2002) ISBN 1-919798-38-2

25 *Zimbabweans Who Move: Perspectives on International Migration in Zimbabwe* (2002) ISBN 1-919798-40-4

26 *The Border Within: The Future of the Lesotho-South African International Boundary* (2002) ISBN 1-919798-41-2

27 *Mobile Namibia: Migration Trends and Attitudes* (2002) ISBN 1-919798-44-7

28 *Changing Attitudes to Immigration and Refugee Policy in Botswana* (2003) ISBN 1-919798-47-1

29 *The New Brain Drain from Zimbabwe* (2003) ISBN 1-919798-48-X

30 *Regionalizing Xenophobia? Citizen Attitudes to Immigration and Refugee Policy in Southern Africa* (2004) ISBN 1-919798-53-6

31 *Migration, Sexuality and HIV/AIDS in Rural South Africa* (2004) ISBN 1-919798-63-3

32 *Swaziland Moves: Perceptions and Patterns of Modern Migration* (2004) ISBN 1-919798-67-6

33 *HIV/AIDS and Children's Migration in Southern Africa* (2004) ISBN 1-919798-70-6

34 *Medical Leave: The Exodus of Health Professionals from Zimbabwe* (2005) ISBN 1-919798-74-9

35 *Degrees of Uncertainty: Students and the Brain Drain in Southern Africa* (2005) ISBN 1-919798-84-6

36 *Restless Minds: South African Students and the Brain Drain* (2005) ISBN 1-919798-82-X

37 *Understanding Press Coverage of Cross-Border Migration in Southern Africa since 2000* (2005) ISBN 1-919798-91-9

38 *Northern Gateway: Cross-Border Migration Between Namibia and Angola* (2005) ISBN 1-919798-92-7

39 *Early Departures: The Emigration Potential of Zimbabwean Students* (2005) ISBN 1-919798-99-4

40 *Migration and Domestic Workers: Worlds of Work, Health and Mobility in Johannesburg* (2005) ISBN 1-920118-02-0

41 *The Quality of Migration Services Delivery in South Africa* (2005) ISBN 1-920118-03-9

42 *States of Vulnerability: The Future Brain Drain of Talent to South Africa* (2006) ISBN 1-920118-07-1

43 *Migration and Development in Mozambique: Poverty, Inequality and Survival* (2006) ISBN 1-920118-10-1

44 *Migration, Remittances and Development in Southern Africa* (2006) ISBN 1-920118-15-2

45 *Medical Recruiting: The Case of South African Health Care Professionals* (2007) ISBN 1-920118-47-0

46 *Voices From the Margins: Migrant Women's Experiences in Southern Africa* (2007) ISBN 1-920118-50-0

47 *The Haemorrhage of Health Professionals From South Africa: Medical Opinions* (2007) ISBN 978-1-920118-63-1

48 *The Quality of Immigration and Citizenship Services in Namibia* (2008) ISBN 978-1-920118-67-9

49 *Gender, Migration and Remittances in Southern Africa* (2008) ISBN 978-1-920118-70-9

50 *The Perfect Storm: The Realities of Xenophobia in Contemporary South Africa* (2008) ISBN 978-1-920118-71-6

51 *Migrant Remittances and Household Survival in Zimbabwe* (2009) ISBN 978-1-920118-92-1

52 *Migration, Remittances and 'Development' in Lesotho* (2010) ISBN 978-1-920409-26-5

53 *Migration-Induced HIV and AIDS in Rural Mozambique and Swaziland* (2011) ISBN 978-1-920409-49-4

54 *Medical Xenophobia: Zimbabwean Access to Health Services in South Africa* (2011) ISBN 978-1-920409-63-0

55 *The Engagement of the Zimbabwean Medical Diaspora* (2011) ISBN 978-1-920409-64-7

56 *Right to the Classroom: Educational Barriers for Zimbabweans in South Africa* (2011) ISBN 978-1-920409-68-5

57 *Patients Without Borders: Medical Tourism and Medical Migration in Southern Africa* (2012) ISBN 978-1-920409-74-6

58 *The Disengagement of the South African Medical Diaspora* (2012) ISBN 978-1-920596-00-2

59 *The Third Wave: Mixed Migration from Zimbabwe to South Africa* (2012) ISBN 978-1-920596-01-9

60 *Linking Migration, Food Security and Development* (2012) ISBN 978-1-920596-02-6

61 *Unfriendly Neighbours: Contemporary Migration from Zimbabwe to Botswana* (2012) ISBN 978-1-920596-16-3

62 *Heading North: The Zimbabwean Diaspora in Canada* (2012) ISBN 978-1-920596-03-3

63 *Dystopia and Disengagement: Diaspora Attitudes Towards South Africa* (2012) ISBN 978-1-920596-04-0

64 *Soft Targets: Xenophobia, Public Violence and Changing Attitudes to Migrants in South Africa after May 2008* (2013) ISBN 978-1-920596-05-7

65 *Brain Drain and Regain: Migration Behaviour of South African Medical Professionals* (2014) ISBN 978-1-920596-07-1

66 *Xenophobic Violence in South Africa: Denialism, Minimalism, Realism* (2014) ISBN 978-1-920596-08-8

67 *Migrant Entrepreneurship Collective Violence and Xenophobia in South Africa* (2014) ISBN 978-1-920596-09-5

68 *Informal Migrant Entrepreneurship and Inclusive Growth in South Africa, Zimbabwe and Mozambique* (2015) ISBN 978-1-920596-10-1

69 *Calibrating Informal Cross-Border Trade in Southern Africa* (2015) ISBN 978-1-920596-13-2

70 *International Migrants and Refugees in Cape Town's Informal Economy* (2016) ISBN 978-1-920596-15-6

71 *International Migrants in Johannesburg's Informal Economy* (2016) ISBN 978-1-920596-18-7

72 *Food Remittances: Migration and Food Security in Africa* (2016) ISBN 978-1-920596-19-4

73 *Informal Entrepreneurship and Cross-Border Trade in Maputo, Mozambique* (2016) ISBN 978-1-920596-20-0

www.ingramcontent.com/pod-product-compliance
Lightning Source LLC
Chambersburg PA
CBHW080135270326
41926CB00021B/4487